Discovering Geography

What Is the Weather Like?

There are many types of weather. It can be hot or cold, wet or dry, windy or calm.

Weather can be rainy, sunny, windy or calm.

Wind is moving air.
Sometimes wind feels hot.
Sometimes it feels cold.

Wind makes this boat move.

Wind can be gentle.

The wind blows sand from this girl's hand.

Wind can be strong.

It is hard to walk in a strong wind.

Clouds can show you what the weather is like.

These clouds show that it is still and sunny.

These clouds show
that it is windy.

These clouds show
that rain is coming.

Rain is water that falls from clouds.

Rain can be heavy or light.

Sunshine makes a place warm.
Sometimes sunshine makes a place very hot.

When it is very cold, water in the clouds can freeze. This makes snow.

A lot of snowflakes fell to cover this playground!

Sometimes rain freezes and makes balls of ice. This is hail.

Hail has fallen on the ground.

In a storm, you might see lightning. Sometimes you will hear loud thunder.

Lightning flashes across a stormy sky.

A cyclone is a storm with very strong winds and heavy rain.

Cyclones can cause a lot of damage.

Some places have four seasons in a year. The weather is different in each season.

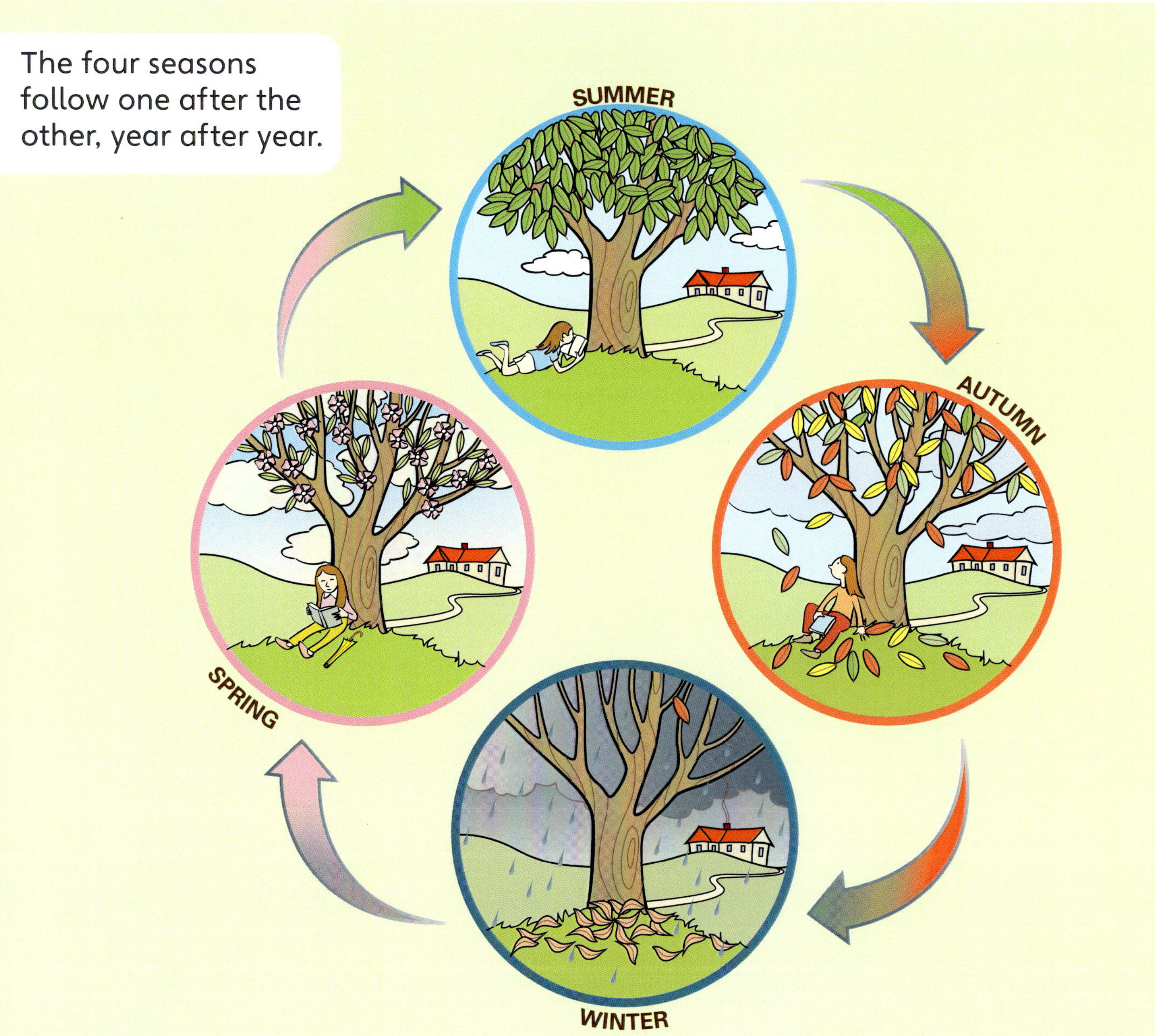

The four seasons follow one after the other, year after year.

In summer, it can be very hot.

In autumn, the weather cools down. Some trees lose their leaves.

In winter, it can be cold.

In spring, it gets warmer and plants can grow.

Some places have only two seasons. These seasons are called the wet season and the dry season.

In the wet season, this water hole is full.

In the dry season, this water hole is dry.

In the dry season, there is very little rain.
The days are hot and sunny.

In the wet season, it is still very hot but it also rains and rains. It can rain for weeks.

When the rains come, they fill the dry creeks. Rivers flow and plants grow again.

Aboriginal people have different seasons. They watch the plants and animals to see what weather is coming.

If you see lizards, it will be sunny and dry. They will hide if it is going to rain.

The Miriwoong people have a hot season, a wet season and a cold season.

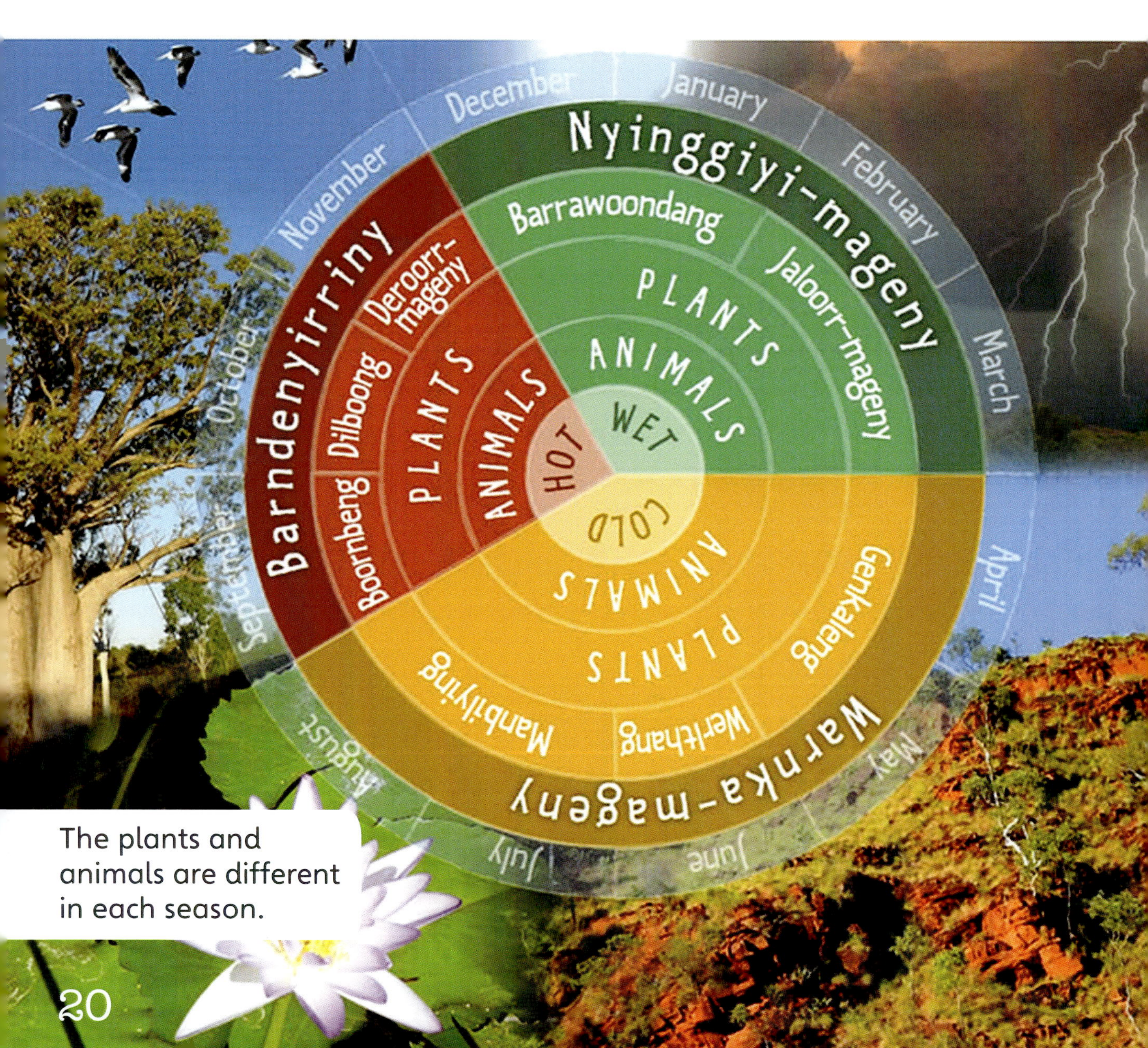

The plants and animals are different in each season.

Sometimes it does not rain for a long time. This is called a drought.

There has not been any rain here for a long time. Plants cannot grow.

Sometimes it rains too much
and the water has nowhere to go.
This is called a flood.

There has been a flood in this street.

Sometimes the sun shines after it rains.
We can see a rainbow.

What is the weather like where you are?